GABRIEL'S
JOURNEY

Nora Rose

Balboa Press books may be ordered through booksellers or by contacting:

Balboa Press
A Division of Hay House
1663 Liberty Drive
Bloomington, IN 47403
www.balboapress.com
1 (877) 407-4847

ISBN: 978-1-5043-4683-2 (sc)
ISBN: 978-1-5043-4682-5 (e)

Library of Congress Control Number: 2015920693

Print information available on the last page.

Balboa Press rev. date: 05/30/2017

BALBOA®
PRESS
A DIVISION OF HAY HOUSE

In memory of my grandfather, Gabriel Iovino, and his desire for a new life and pursuit of happiness. Thank you for enriching the Italian-American culture in our family. You continue to inspire me.

Dear Parents, Teachers, and Coaches,

I'm excited to share this book with you and your children. Writing the story of my grandfather, Gabriel Iovino, was a fascinating experience that took on a life of its own. Because of his story, learning about the struggles and joys that many Europeans experienced while traveling to America has touched my heart much more than just reading history books about that time.

While writing this book, I learned what a strong, courageous, determined man my grandfather was. Also, I visited the Statue of Liberty site, which is spectacular. I spent days on that site, researching information. I also called Ellis Island, where the staff was indescribably helpful. Reading original documents was also an incredible experience.

We have all immigrated from somewhere. Where did your family history originate?

I trained for a year with Jack Canfield and read his book *The Success Principles: How to Get from Where You Are to Where You Want to Be*. And I use his concepts "Believe in Yourself" and "Know What You Want" to enhance *Gabriel's Journey*.

I have taught at Our Lady of Lourdes School, Chicago; Walker School, Evanston, Illinois; and B. J. Hooper School, Lindenhurst, Illinois. I also have been a substitute teacher at several schools in southeast Wisconsin.

Please help me teach others about The Success Principles. You don't have to be a master of the principles to lead a discussion group. You just have to be willing to facilitate a discussion in your family, club, or church group, with coworkers, or in a company in which people would like to work together to support each other in actively living these principles. The results will be miraculous! And you could be the person who makes it happen.

I envision a world where all people are inspired to believe in themselves and their abilities and will be empowered to reach their full potential. They can visualize their dreams like my grandfather did in *Gabriel's Journey*.

We all like to listen and to tell stories. The stories we tell ourselves make all the difference in the life we create for ourselves. My dream is that each one of us comes to recognize and connect to the amazing gifts inside ourselves so we can live positive, fulfilling lives that we share with others.

Nora Rose

In 1915, Italy entered World War I and so did my older brother. Every day I woke up for school wondering if I would be called to join the war. Every day I thought about my cousin's family in America. I could only imagine the "land of the free" called America and all its good fortune.

After school, my brother, two sisters, and I helped on the farm—except for the day I started a job after school in a factory that made supplies for the war. I did that for three years and finished school. When the war ended, so did my job.

My brother never came home. More than three hundred thousand men died in that war. Tears streamed down my parents' faces as I hugged them tightly. For years we had shared every detail of our lives. We had helped each other deal with the pain, suffering, and joy that happen in a family with five children.

What do I want? I thought about that every night before I went to sleep. *What do I want to do, to be, to have?* My remaining brother lay near me. We would talk about what we wanted. I wanted a job. I wanted a family. I wanted to go to America. I believed I could go to the land of opportunity. I talked about it with my family, and I had the money to buy my ticket. I said I would send for my brother after I arrived safely.

In March 1920, I hugged my mother, father, brother, and two sisters good-bye. Friends and family wished me *buon viaggio* (a good trip). I left Naples, Italy, and boarded a ship named *Canada*.

Aboard the ship, it was very crowded. Some people read books, some talked, some prayed, some played music. Some traveled as families, but many were alone like me.

During the day, I spent my time above deck, looking out into the deep blue sea. Surrounded by water, I thought about Scisciano (pronounced *she shano*), the little town I had left behind, and the promising future of America.

As the sun set, it became very cold. I pulled my coat tighter and held onto my hat.

Below deck is where everyone slept. My suitcase was placed outside the cabin door. I shared a room with a fifteen-year-old boy. There was a twin bed on each side of the tiny room and a small dresser in between with a light.

"Hi, I am James," he said. "I am going to Syracuse, New York, to live with my cousin Anophrio."

"I'm Gabriel. I'm going to stop in New York and then take a sixteen-hour train ride to Chicago, Illinois, to live with my cousin."

As we shook hands, I said, "*Paisano*," which means "friend" in Italian.

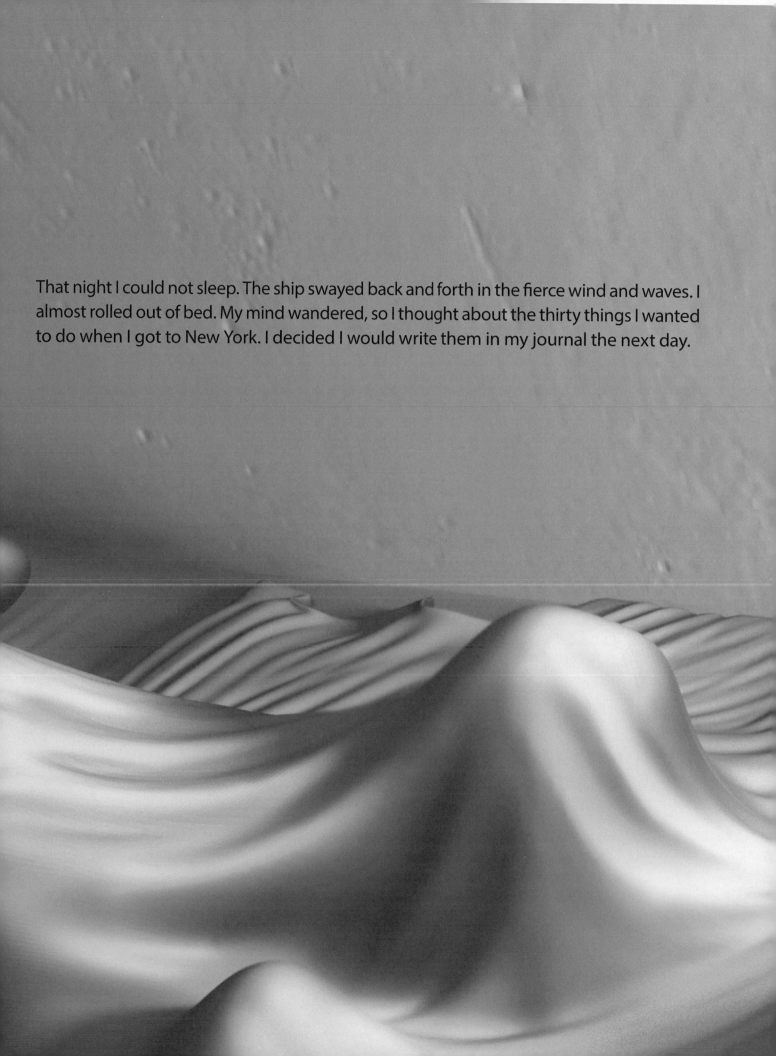

That night I could not sleep. The ship swayed back and forth in the fierce wind and waves. I almost rolled out of bed. My mind wandered, so I thought about the thirty things I wanted to do when I got to New York. I decided I would write them in my journal the next day.

30 le cose che voglio fa[r]
a New York

1. vedere la statua della libe[rtà]

2. A piedi a Wall Street

3. Visitare un cugino

4. Vedere il Chrysler Buildin[g]

5. As[colta]tare una radio

The sun rose, and I went up to the outside deck for some fresh air. I looked out into the ocean for a while. Then I found a spot to sit and write in my journal. I wrote down the thirty things I wanted to do in New York, the thirty things I wanted to do in Chicago, the thirty things I wanted to have, and the thirty things I wanted to do before I died. This was a way for me to get started in my new country.

Then it was time to eat. Everyone sat at a long, wooden table to eat spaghetti and bread. One night there was lasagna, but not like my mother's. After the fourth night, it didn't matter what food was served, because not many were eating.

A severe storm rolled in that night. The ship bobbed up and down and lunged forward and back. The sea splashed over the boat and across the top deck. All the passengers had to stay in their cabins, and people were getting sick. It smelled awful! Babies cried. Children screamed. Someone shouted, "We're all going to die!" Another called, "*Zia!*" (Auntie).

James said his stomach felt like it was in his throat. He looked as white as a sheet—not well at all. I found him some water and told him to think about docking in New York. We took deep breaths to calm down and relax.

Day followed night, and night followed day. Finally, the storm passed, and James and I ran up the steps to the top deck for some fresh, salty air. I held my face to the sky and said, "Thank You," and James did the same. We sat in silence for a little while.

I asked James if he wanted to play a game called "I Want." Since we didn't have a pen and paper to write the answers down, we just said them out loud. To play the game, we ask each other, "What do you want?" "What do you want?" and we each said what we wanted. "I want to take a shower." "I want fresh water." "I want to wash my clothes." "I want a wife." "I want someone to love me." "I want a house." "I want to make a difference."

We laughed and then sat in silence for a few minutes, thinking about what we valued. Then we sat longer, listening to the music someone played as we thought about what we loved that we had left behind.

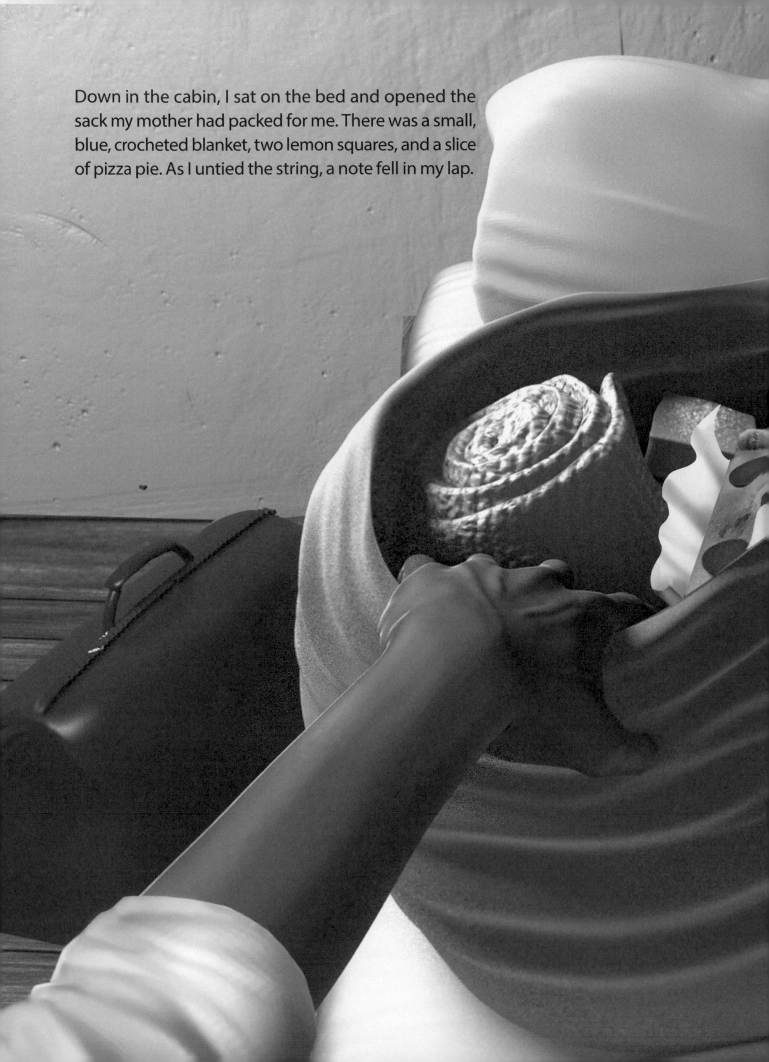

Down in the cabin, I sat on the bed and opened the sack my mother had packed for me. There was a small, blue, crocheted blanket, two lemon squares, and a slice of pizza pie. As I untied the string, a note fell in my lap.

Dear Gabriel

By now you know how much we miss you.
Contact us when you are safely with your cousins.

We love you.

Mom and Dad

I took a bite of the lemon square and held the flavor in my mouth. It was so good. Just then James walked into the cabin. "Here, have a lemon square. My mother sent it," I said as I handed it to him. He smiled and took a bite. I saved the pizza for later.

"This destination feels right, James," I said. "We have traveled a long way. We will live a balanced and successful life." We talked about our visions for work, career, finances, recreation, free time, health, relationships and family, goals, and how we would live in our community. We had no idea how any of it would happen. We just knew that it was going to happen in America. We sat thinking about a bright future.

Suddenly we heard the sound of loud music with people clapping and singing. So we went up to the top deck, where people were dancing. Everyone was smiling and happy.

"We are almost there!" someone shouted.

"There is land!" said another.

"Merica!" shouted another.

We clapped our hands to the music, excited that we'd had a safe voyage.

The next day, everyone waited to be called off the boat. Then everyone hurried off to stand in crowded lines. People were pointing at a statue. "There she is!" someone shouted. I turned to look at the Statue of Liberty standing so tall and proud and free. I had a tingling feeling throughout my body as I looked at her through the sunlight and said, "Thank you."

Some people were kneeling and others were pointing at the beautiful lady and at the building with the flag.

I gave James a hug. "We are moving in the right direction. You have my address. Good luck to you."

Flags waved, horns blew, and people cheered and waved with excitement. Family members called out, "Sergie! Lena! Patrick!" to welcome them. I didn't have anyone waiting for me or calling my name, but I had believed I could make the trip, and I was there for *me*.

It was my turn to register. "Welcome to Ellis Island. What is your name?" asked the inspector.

I said my name in Italian: "Gabriel Iovino."

He wrote, "Jovane, Gabriele." Then he measured me and said, "Five six." He looked at my eyes and wrote, "Chestnut." He looked at my face and wrote, "Fair complexion and in good health." Then he wrote, "1920, 18 years old."

He asked where I was going. "1122 Polk Street, Chicago," I replied, adding that I was staying in New York a few days and then going to Chicago by train.

He showed me where to buy the train ticket.

I had passed inspection! I had done it! I stood tall and proud in America with the vision of my big dreams inside me.

PASSENGER RECORD

American Family Immigration History Center® at Ellis Island

First Name : Gabriele

Last Name : Jovane

Nationality : Italy, Italian South

Last Place of Residence : Scisciano Cas., Italy

Date of Arrival : Mar 05, 1920

Age at Arrival : 18y

Gender : Male

Marital Status : Single

Ship of Travel : Canada

Port of Departure : Naples

Manifest Line Number : 0019

ELLIS ISLAND

The Statue of Liberty-Ellis Island Foundation, Inc.

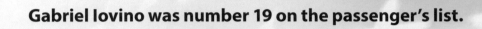

LIST OR MANIFEST OF ALIEN PASSENGERS FOR THE UNITED

ALL ALIENS arriving at a port of continental United States from a foreign port or a port of the insular possessions of the United States, and all aliens arriving at a port of said insular possessions from a foreign port, a port of continental United
This (white) sheet is for the listing of

S. S. CANADA   Passengers sailing from NAPLES on the 20th DAY of FEBRUARY, 1920

No. on List	HEAD-TAX STATUS	Family name	Given name	Age Yrs.	Mos.	Sex	Married or single	Calling or occupation	Able to— Read	Read what language	Write	Nationality (Country of which citizen or subject)	Race or people	Last permanent residence. Country	City or town	The name and complete address of nearest relative or friend in country whence alien came	Final destination State	City or town
1		DE NICHILO	GIUSEPPE	24		m	s	unson	yes	Italian	yes	Italy	soitalian	Italy	Molfetta Bari	her father Leonardo De Michile Molfetta Bari	N.Y.	Hoboken
2		SGAVA	FRANCESCO SAVERIO	27		m	s	sailor	yes	italian	yes	Italy	soitalian	Italy	do	his wife Campo Beatrice Molfetta Bari	do	do
3		ANDRIULO	MAURO	38		m	s	unson	yes	italian	yes	Italy	soitalian	Italy	do	his mother De Bari Elisabetta Molfetta Bari	do	do
4		ALLEGRETTA	LEONARDO	36		m	m	peasant	yes	italian	yes	Italy	soitalian	Italy	do	his wife Dorotea Brunetti Molfetta Bari	do	do
5		DE PALMA	MICHELE	34		m	m	peasant	yes	italian	yes	Italy	soitalian	Italy	do	his wife Sabolla Angela Cantatore Mofetta Bari	do	do
6		ANGIONE	ANTONIO	40		m	m	peasant	yes	italian	yes	Italy	soitalian	Italy	do	his wife Marca Scardiglia Molfetta Bari	do	Hudson Fols
7		PAPPAGALLO	MAURO	40		m	m	peasant	yes	italian	yes	Italy	soitalian	Italy	do	his wife Elisabetta Pappagallo Molfetta Bari	do	Hoboken
8		AMATO	GIUSEPPE	27		m	s	work	yes	italian	yes	Italy	soitalian	Italy	S.Martino V.C.	his father Giuseppe Amato S.Martino V.C.	Conn.	New Haven
9		TORTORA	GIOSUE	28		m	s	waiter	yes	italian	yes	Italy	soitalian	Italy	Saviano Caserta	his father Felice Saviano Saviano Caserta	N.Y.	Brooklyn
10	REMITTED	Miele	Bartolomeo	63		m	w	barber	no	rejoins his son		Italy	soitalian	U.S.A.	New-York	his nephew Grassi Mariantonia Tufino Caserta	do	New-York
11		SABINO	GIOVANNI	27		m	s	peasant	yes	italian	yes	Italy	soitalian	Italy	Pietramelara	his father Giuseppe Sabino Pietramelara Caserta	Ill.	Chicago
12		SABINO	MARIA	18		f	s	peasant	yes	italian	yes	Italy	soitalian	Italy	do	her father Giuseppe Sabino Pietramelara Caserta	do	do
13		DI DONATO	CATERINA	46		w		house-wife	no	rejoins her husband		italy	soitalian	Italy	S.Antimo Napoli	his brother Carlo Di Donato S.Antimo Napoli	N.Y.	New-York
14		son DIANTONIO	FELICE	16		m	s	laborer	yes	italian	yes	Italy	soitalian	Italy	do	his uncle	do	do
15		son do	PEPPINO	13		m	s	do	no	do	yes	Italy	soitalian	Italy	do	his uncle	do	do
16		daughter do	MARIA									Italy	soitalian	Italy	do	her uncle	do	do
17	19	JOVANE	GABRIELE									soitalian	Italy	Medugno Bari	his wife Stella Anna Medugno Bari		Syracuse
19		JOVANE	GABRIELE	18		m	s	peasant	yes	italian	yes	Italy	soitalian	Italy	Scisciano Cas.	his father Francesco Jovane Scisciano Caserta	Ill.	Chicago
20		GRANDOLFO	AGOSTINO	19		m	s	do	yes	italian	yes	Italy	soitalian	Italy	Bitritto Bari	his father Emanuele Grandolfo Bitritto Bari	do	do
21		DELIOIO	LEOPOLDO	18		m	s	do	yes	italian	yes	Italy	soitalian	Italy	do	his father Michele Deligio Bitritto Bari	Colo.	Denver
22		BAVARO	VITO FIORE	20		m	s	do	yes	italian	yes	Italy	soitalian	Italy	do	his father Pietro Bavaro Bitritto Bari	Ill.	Chicago
23		RUBINO	DOMENICO	19		m	s	do	yes	italian	yes	Italy	soitalian	Italy	do	his father Pasquale Rubino Bitritto Bari	Nevada	Kimberly
24		CIUFO	RAFFAELE	17		m	s	do	yes	italian	yes	Italy	soitalian	Italy	do	his mother Calabrese Maria Bitritto Bari	do	do
25		FRANCONE	VINCENZO	20		m	s	do	yes	italian and english	yes	Italy	soitalian	Italy	do	his mother Francone Bitritto Bari	Utah	Salt Lake City
26		D'AMBROSIO	VITO GIUSEPPE	18		m	s	do	yes	italian	yes	Italy	soitalian	Italy	do	his father Domenico Antonio D'Ambrosio Bitritto Bari	Ill.	Chicago
27		MAFFEI	LUIGI	18		m	s	do	yes	italian	yes	Italy	soitalian	Italy	do	his mother Lucarelli Carmela Bitritto Bari		
28		URSINI	MICHELE	22		m	s	do	yes	italian	yes	Italy	soitalian	Italy	do	his mother Deligio Maria Bitritto Bari	Ill.	Chicago
29		VALLONE	GIUSEPPE	17		m	s	do	yes	italian	yes	Italy	soitalian	Italy	do	his father Raffaele Vallone Bitritto Bari	do	do
30		BAVARO	MICHELE	23		m	s	do	yes	italian	yes	Italy	soitalian	Italy	do	his father Bavaro Bitritto Bari	do	do

30

Total passengers 19
U. S. citizens . . . . . .
Aliens . . . . . .

* Permanent residence within the meaning of this manifest shall be actual or intended residence of one year or more.
† List of races will be found on the back of this sheet.

List **6**
The entries on this sheet must be typewritten or printed.

States, or a port of another insular possession, in whatsoever class they travel, MUST be fully listed and the master or commanding officer of each vessel carrying such passengers must upon arrival deliver lists thereof to the immigration officer. STEERAGE PASSENGERS ONLY

Arriving at Port of __NEW-YORK__ , *on the 5th march* , 19**2**0

57

No. on List	15 Whether having a ticket to final destination	16 By whom was passage paid?	17 Whether in possession of $50, and if less, how much?	18 Whether ever before in the United States; and if so, when and where?		19 Whether going to join a relative or friend; and if so, what relative or friend, and his name and complete address.	20 Purpose of coming to United States	21	22	23	24 Whether an anarchist	25	26	27 Whether able to read/write	28 Condition of health, mental and physical.	Deformed or crippled. Nature, length of time, and cause.	29 Height Feet	30 Inches	31 Color of—		32 Marks of identification.	33 Place of birth.	
				Yes or No.	Year or period of years. Where?													Hair	Eyes	Compl.		Country	City or town
1	no	himself	25	no	—	his cousin Corrado Mancini 314- 6th St. Hoboken N.Y.	no	always	yes	no	no	no		no	no	good	no	5	10	brow.	brow.	chest.		Italy	Melfetta Bari
2	no	himself	25	no	—	his cousin Domenico Ambone Department esta Hoboken N.Y.	no	always	yes	no	no	no		no	no	good	no	5	8	fair	brow.	chest.		Italy	do
3	no	himself	25	no	—	his brother Michele De Candia Hoboken N.Y.	no	always	yes	no	no	no		no	no	good	no	5	5	fair	brow.	chest.		Italy	do
4	no	himself	25	yes/909/911 N.Y.		his cousin Allegretto Nicola St. No 346 Hoboken N.Y.	no	always	yes	no	no	no		no	no	good	no	5	8	fair	brow.	chest.	—	Italy	do
5	no	himself	25	yes 912/915 Hobo		his cousin Giovannangelo La Candia Hoboken N.Y.	no	always	yes	no	no	no		no	no	good	no	5	4	fair	brow.	chest.		Italy	do
6	no	himself	25			his cousin Palmietti Sebastiano Box 100 Hudson Fels N.Y.	no	always	yes	no	no	no		no	no	good	no	5	5	brow.	brow.	chest.	—	Italy	do
7	no	himself	25	yes 911/914 Hobo		his cousin Giuseppe Mele 11V Adams St. Hoboken N.Y.	undetermined		—	no	no	no		no	no	good	no	5	5	fair	brow.	sky-b.	—	Italy	do
8	no	himself		yes 912/915 Hobo		his cousin Pasquale Picaniello Wester St. No 69 New-Haven Conn.	undetermined		—	no	no	no		no	no	good	no	5	6	brow.	brow.	chest.		Italy	S. Martino V.
9	no	himself	30	no		his uncle Luigi Scotto 176 Bacrun St. B'lyn N.Y.	undetermined		—	no	no	no		no	no	good	no	5	11	fair	brow.	chest.		Italy	Saviano Caser
10	no	himself	762	yes 895/919 N.Y.		his son Sebastiano Mele 716 bedford Ave B'lyn N,Y.	undetermined		—	no	no	no		no	no	good	no	5	3	fair	grey	dark	—	Italy	Roccarainola
11	no	himself	100	yes 895/919 Chicago		his brother-in-law Filippe Serghts 258 E. 22 St. Chicago Ill.	undetermined		—	no	no	no		no	no	good	no	5	4	fair	brow.	chest.		Italy	do
12	no	herself	100	no		her brother-in-law Filippo DiaBere Sterght. 258 E. 22 St. Chicago Ill.	undetermined		—	no	no	no		no	no	good	no	5	6	fair	brow.	chest.		Italy	do
13	no	herself	40	yes 902/908 N.Y.		her husband Giulio D'Antenio 16 Peke St. Carberr N.Y.	undetermined		—	no	no	no		no	no	good	no	5	4	fair	blak	blak		Italy	S. Antimo Napa
14		his mother				his father	undetermined		—	no	no	no		no	no	good	no			brow.	blak	blak		U.S.A	New-York
15		his mother				his father	undetermined		—	no	no	no		no	no	good	no							U.S.A	New-York
16		her mother				her father	do		—	no	no	no		no	no	good	no							Italy	S.Antimo Napa
17		her mother				her father	do		—	no	no	no		no	no	good	no							Italy	do
18	no	himself	25	yes 905/908 Syracuse		his father Bellino Giuseppe Braid St. 205 Syracuse N.Y.	no	always	yes	no	no	no		no	no	good	no	5	7	fair	brow.	dark		Italy	Madugno Bari
19	no	himself	100	—		his brother Onofrio Jevane 1122 W. Folk St. Chicago Ill.	no	always	yes	no	no	no		no	no	good	no	5	6	fair	brow.	chest.		Italy	Suisulane
20	no	himself	100	no	—	his brother Grandolfo Luigi No1120 Grand Ave Chicago Ill.	no	always	yes	no	no	no		no	no	good	no	5	3	brow.	brow.	dark		Italy	Bitritto
21	no	himself	100	no	—	his cousin Albanese Domenico No 726 -W.- 38 St. Denver Colorado	undetermined		yes	no	no	no		no	no	good	no	5	6	fair	brow.	sky-b.	—	Italy	do
22	no	himself	760	no	—	his cousin Pantaleo Nicola 952 - Grand Ave Chicago Ill.	undetermined		yes	no	no	no		no	no	good	no	5	6	brow.	brow.	chest.	—	Italy	do
23	no	himself	760	no	—	his uncle Ginfie Domenico Box 17 Kimberly Nevada	no	always	yes	no	no	no		no	no	good	no	5	6	fair	brow.	chest.		Italy	do
24	no	himself	760	no	—	his father Ciufo Domenico Box 17	undetermined		—	no	no	no		no	no	good	no	5	6	brow.	blak	sky-b.	—	Italy	do
25	no	himself	700	yes 913/919 N.Y.		his uncle Francene Pasquale No 301 W. 3rd South Salt Lake Utah	undetermined		¾	no	no	no		no	no	good	no	5	6	fair	brow.	dark	—	Italy	do
26	no	himself	760	no	—	his uncle Taccogna Francesco No 952 - Grand Ave Chicago Ill.	undetermined		yes	no	no	no		no	no	good	no	5	8	fair	brow.	chest.		Italy	do
27	no	himself	100	no	—	his uncle Michele Maffei Box 328 Ruth Nevada	no	always	yes	no	no	no		no	no	good	no	5	6	fair	brow.	chest.		Italy	do
28	no	himself	100	no	—	his cousin Vallone Giovanni West Grand Avenue No 1120 Chicago Ill.	undetermined		no	no	no	no		no	no	good	no	5	3	fair	brow.	chest.		Italy	do
29	no	himself	100	no	—	his brother Vallone Giovanni 1120 West. Carnd Ave Chicago Ill.	no	always	yes	no	no	no		no	no	good	no	4	7	fair	brow.	chest.		Italy	do
30	no	himself	100	no	—	his brother-in-law Taccogna Francesco No 932 - West Grand Ave Chicago Ill.	no	always	yes	no	no	no		no	no	good	no	5	7	fair	brow.	chest.		Italy	do

Note.—Full text of question 24 is as follows: Whether a person who believes in or advocates the overthrow by force or violence of the Government of the United States or of all forms of law, or who disbelieves in or is opposed to organized government, or who advocates the assassination of public officials, or who advocates or teaches the unlawful destruction of property, or is a member of or affiliated with any organization entertaining and teaching disbelief in or opposition to organized government or which teaches the unlawful destruction of property, or who advocates or teaches the duty, necessity, or propriety of the unlawful assaulting or killing of any officer or officers, either of specific individuals or of officers generally, of the Government of the United States or of any other organized government because of his or their official character.

Vision Exercise

Put on some relaxing music and sit in a comfortable environment. Close your eyes and think about what your ideal life would look like if you could have it exactly the way you want it.

How much money do you want to have? What does your house look like? What color are the walls? What kind of yard do you want? Does it have a pool or horses? Fill in all the details.

What is your ideal job? Where are you working? What are you doing?

How will you spend your free time? What hobbies are you doing, and what fun are you having with your family and friends?

What does your body look like? How are you exercising to stay healthy? What healthy foods are you eating and drinking? Do you drink a lot of water?

What is your relationship with your family like? Who are your friends? Do these friendships feel loving, kind, supportive, empowering?

What do you want to learn in school? Do you want to go to college, learn a trade, attend a workshop, get therapy, grow spiritually, meditate, play an instrument, write a book, run a marathon, take an art class, travel?

What does your community look like? What activities does it provide? What do you do to help others and make a difference? Who are you helping?

Think about all of these.

The Know-What-You-Want Vision Board

The idea behind a vision board is that when you surround yourself with images of who you want to become, what you want to have, and where you want to live or vacation, your life changes to match those images and those desires.

Items needed: poster board or large piece of cardboard, glue sticks, scissors, magazines.

1. Have fun looking through the magazines and cutting out pictures or words that show what you want. (You might make a birthday board, a Happy New Year board, or a vacation board. You might want to become a cheerleader or a basketball player. You might want a new bike, a new car, a new house. You get the idea.)
2. Go through the images and lay your favorites on the board. You might have a theme. Be creative.
3. Glue your pictures and words onto the board.
4. Put your vision board in a place where you can see it every day. Look at your vision board for one to two minutes every day for as long as it takes to live your vision.
5. After you achieve that goal, make a new vision board. Have fun with this.

Passport Activity

Are you ready to take a journey through your imagination? Make a passport to take with you on all your favorite adventures. Passports allow people to travel all over the world to meet new people and see new places. Use your passport to take you to all your favorite places. Create a stamp for each country you want to visit. Color them. Glue them on your passport. Add more pages. Put your picture on your passport too. Happy travels!

Printed in the United States
By Bookmasters